Dear Parents,

Welcome to the Scholastic Reader series. We have taken over 90 years of experience with teachers, parents, and children and put it into a program that is designed to match your child's interests and skills.

Level 1—Short sentences and stories made up of words kids can sound out using their phonics skills and words that are important to remember.

Level 2—Longer sentences and stories with words kids need to know and new "big" words that they will want to know.

Level 3—From sentences to paragraphs to longer stories, these books have large "chunks" of text and are made up of a rich vocabulary.

Level 4—First chapter books with more words and fewer pictures.

It is important that children learn to read well enough to succeed in school and beyond. Here are ideas for reading this book with your child:

- Look at the book together. Encourage your child to read the title and make a prediction about the story.
- Read the book together. Encourage your child to sound out words when appropriate. When your child struggles, you can help by providing the word.
- Encourage your child to retell the story. This is a great way to check for comprehension.

Scholastic Readers are designed to support your child's efforts to learn how to read at every age and every stage. Enjoy helping your child learn to read and love to read.

　　　　—**Francie Alexander**
　　　　　　Chief Education Officer
　　　　　　Scholastic Education

Ms. Frizzle

Liz

Written by Elizabeth Smith
Illustrated by Carolyn Bracken

Based on *The Magic School Bus* books
written by Joanna Cole and illustrated by Bruce Degen

The author would like to thank George Burgess, Director of the Florida
Program for Shark Research at the Florida Museum of Natural History, for
his help in preparing this book.

ISBN-13: 978-0-545-03464-7
ISBN-10: 0-545-03464-7

12 11 10 9 8   10 11 12 13 14/0

Designed by Rick DeMonico

First printing, November 2007   40   Printed in the U.S.A.

The Magic School Bus
and the Shark Adventure

Arnold Ralphie Keesha Phoebe Carlos Tim Wanda Dorothy Ann

Cartwheel
·B·O·O·K·S·®

SCHOLASTIC INC.

New York Toronto London Auckland Sydney
Mexico City New Delhi Hong Kong Buenos Aires

We have fun in Ms. Frizzle's class.
Ms. Frizzle wears funny clothes.

"Can I paint this?" Keesha asks.
"I found it at the beach."
We look at what Keesha found.
No one knows what it is.

"We'll find out what Keesha's mermaid purse is," Ms. Frizzle says.
"To the bus!"

Ms. Frizzle drives us to the shore.
We go right up to the water.

The bus drives into the water.
It grows fins and gills.
Now it's the Magic School Fish!

There is a lot to see underwater.
"I see sharks and fish!" says Ralphie.
"Sharks *are* fish," Ms. Frizzle tells us.

Ms. Frizzle drives close to a shark so we can see it better.

NURSE SHARK
7 - 9 FT LONG

NOT JUST ANOTHER FISH!
by Tim

Sharks have gills, fins, and scales like fish. But they are different, too. Sharks' scales are little, hard bumps. Shark skeletons are not made of bone. They are made of cartilage — the stuff you can feel in your ears and in the tip of your nose.

The bus-fish swims deeper into the ocean.
Something huge swims above us.
It's a whale shark!
"Don't worry," says D.A.
"That shark won't hurt us!"

A WHALE OF A SHARK
by Phoebe

A whale shark is the biggest fish in the world, but it eats the smallest food — just tiny plants and shellfish called plankton.

PLANKTON

WHALE SHARK
UP TO 60 FEET

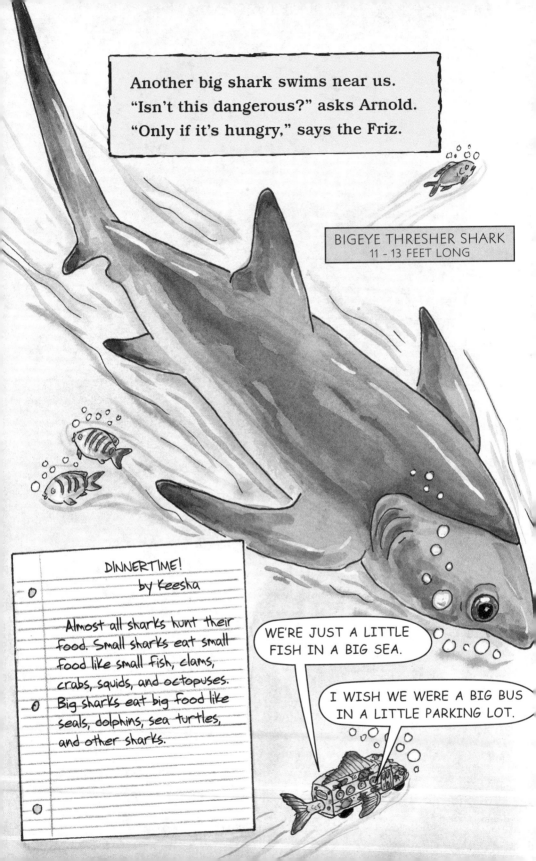

We all look at the lemon shark's teeth.
They are long and sharp.
"When a front tooth falls out," the Friz says,
"one from the row behind will fill its place."

Then the lemon shark turns on us.
"I think this shark *is* hungry," says the Friz.
We have to get away!
The bus dives deep and fast!

We hide in the thick seaweed.
The shark swims away after a different fish.
There are a lot of animals in the seaweed.
The Friz gives us scuba masks.
We put them on and swim out of the bus.

We see something funny in the sand.
"That's a chain dogfish," the Friz tells us.

We swim out to the open water.
A school of hammerhead sharks swims by.
"They hunt at night," D.A. reads from her book.
"So they won't bother us now."

SCALLOPED HAMMERHEAD SHARK
5 - 8 1/2 FEET LONG

Back in the seaweed we see something else —
lots of mermaid's purses!
Tiny sharks swim out of some of them.
Now we know what the purses are!

THE PURSES ARE SHARK EGG CASES!

THAT'S EGG-CELLENT!

We watch the baby sharks swim away.
"Where are their mothers?" Keesha asks.
"Baby sharks take care of themselves,"
says the Friz.

Now it is time to go back to school.
We swim back to the bus-fish.

We get to shore quickly.
The bus becomes a bus again
and we drive back to school.

At school, we finish our picture.
Keesha paints a shark pup.
Arnold draws shark egg cases.
We can't wait to go on another trip!

All sharks use their teeth for hunting, but they use them in different ways.

Great white shark teeth
Used for cutting through big animals
1-1/4 – 2 inches

Lemon shark teeth
Used to spear octopus and small fish
Up to 1 inch

Nurse shark teeth
Used to grind crabs and sea urchins
Up to 1/2 inch

HOW MANY MERMAID'S PURSES DID YOU FIND? IF YOU COUNTED 13, THEN YOU FOUND THEM ALL!